Sunrise Devotions

VOLUME 2

Compiled by
Tim Stearman

Beacon Hill Press of Kansas City
Kansas City, Missouri

Cover Design: Crandall Vail

10 9 8 7 6 5 4 3 2 1

Preface

Thirteen years ago a volume of devotional thoughts for retirees was published under the title *Sunrise Devotions*. The unique feature of that book was that it was written not only for retirees but also by retirees.

Since that time, ministry to older adults has literally exploded. The reason is simple. Today, life expectancy at birth is 70 years for men and 78 years for women. One of every nine persons in the United States is an older adult. By the year 2000, one of every six will be 65 or older. The church has no members who are more faithful, loyal, or generous than this crowd who have given so much to so many for so long.

Because older adults have experienced so much, they have special insights that only time can produce. How appropriate to offer another volume of devotional thoughts gleaning wisdom from the perspective of the older adult.

So once again we are pleased to introduce a volume of devotions for retirees written by retirees. I hope you enjoy *Sunrise Devotions, Volume 2.*

—TIM STEARMAN

Currently Tim Stearman is senior pastor of Tulsa, Okla., Central Church of the Nazarene. He formerly served as director of Adult Ministries in the Sunday School Ministries Division at the denomination's headquarters.

Caleb . . . hath wholly followed the Lord.
(DEUT. 1:36)

Victory Over the Giants

Caleb was 85. That in itself poses some problems. Those of us who approach his age level recognize the tokens of mortality in our joints and bones. It is a little difficult to be immortal in a mortal world.

Caleb was a realist. He did not deny the existence of giants in the land where God placed him. He knew they were there. Big as life! *But:*

1. He had no reservations in his consecration, giants or no giants.

2. He had signed the bottom line of an unconditional contract.

3. He agreed, in advance, to God's terms.

4. He resorted to no self-pity.

5. He looked through and beyond the giants; he saw possibilities, not problems.

6. He was more God-conscious than man-conscious.

We seniors face troubles as big as giants. To name a few possibilities: abandonment, bereavement, loneliness, poverty, rejection, sickness, sorrow. Shall we allow the giants to obscure God? Let's say with Caleb that the giants "are bread for us" (Num. 14:9).

DALLAS BAGGETT
Decatur, Ala.
Pastor, District Superintendent, Evangelist

A dinner was given in Jesus' honor. Martha served, while Lazarus was among those reclining at the table with him.
(JOHN 12:2, NIV)

In Jesus' Honor

Jesus did not have better friends than Martha, Mary, and Lazarus—two sisters and their brother. They loved Jesus dearly, and He was always a welcome guest in their home.

A few days before His death Jesus arrived at their home in Bethany. On this occasion Martha prepared and served a meal in His honor. Mary had a container of perfumed ointment she used in massaging His feet, then she wiped His feet with her hair. She remained in His presence in worship. Lazarus sat at the table with them while the food was served.

Judas criticized the act of Mary and objected to the extravagance in pouring the ointment on Jesus. Many people came through curiosity to observe.

A few days later news came of Jesus' arrest and crucifixion. Martha was glad she served Jesus. Mary was encouraged by her act of kindness. Lazarus was inspired by the memory of his fellowship with Jesus.

Today it is our privilege to serve, worship, and identify with Jesus.

BUFORD BATTIN
El Paso, Tex.
Pastor, Evangelist

Do not cast me away when I am old.
(PS. 71:9, NIV)

Living on the Shelf

Shelf living is frustrating, discouraging. For years you have been in the center of action in church life, but now you are not asked to serve even on a committee. A younger generation has taken over. They have thrown out all those carefully conceived programs you and others worked so hard to develop. The church traditions you loved are forgotten.

What is the remedy for such frustration? The Psalmist has the answer: "They will still bear fruit in old age, they will stay fresh and green" (92:14, NIV). The seasons of life change, but with each season there are opportunities and challenges. It is right that a younger generation should have its opportunity to lead the church.

Now there are new opportunities for us who seem to be on the shelf. We can enter into a ministry of intercession that we didn't have time for when we were so busy. We can minister to other seniors, some of whom are lonely and hurting. We can become grandparents to children at church from nonchurch homes. Let's get off the shelf and "bear fruit in old age."

ALPIN P. BOWES
Prairie Village, Kans.
Minister

He shall see of the travail of his soul, and shall be satisfied: by his knowledge shall my righteous servant justify many.

(ISA. 53:11)

And they were all filled with the Holy Ghost.

(ACTS 2:4)

A Consortium of Saints

For pure entertainment no circus could ever excel camp meeting where Uncle Bud Robinson, T. W. Willingham, Raymond Browning (my father), and Grandmas Cheek and Buss (Olivetians) were present. In all great camps and revivals there is that consortium of saints that insure "the fire will fall."

It was the awesome reality of the presence of the Lord in those shining saints that drew me into the love of Christ and transformed my fascination into genuine change. The Master's touch deep within set the direction of my life. The seeds and superscription of His image were on my soul. And in this better way there will always come the better day.

As Jesus announces Open House for all nations, kindreds, people, and tongues, I have been one of His witnesses, seeing whole congregations sanctified in a single act of God's amazing grace. This is the great satisfaction of the travail of the Savior.

The precious blood of God's own Son has saved and sanctified a wondrous people for His name, and they are called the Bride. Though here neglected and despised, one day the Lamb will bring His chosen ones within the gates, and that's worth everything.

DAVID BROWNING
Rocky Mount, N.C.
Missionary

My kingdom is not of this world.
(JOHN 18:36)

Tickets to the Kingdom

There are conditions of entrance into the heavenly kingdom: new birth, John 3:3; faith and love, James 2:5; humility, Matt. 5:3; and endurance, Acts 14:22.

My Grandmother Baldridge was "Granny" to everyone who knew her, and a real saint who lived 96 years. She owned and operated a boardinghouse, cooking and packing lunches for several men who worked at the steel mill. She did her own cleaning, laundry, etc., and still had time to piece quilts as a hobby. Her love for God was as deep as the ocean, and her faith was as immovable as the Rock of Gibraltar.

She hadn't felt well and stayed indoors a few days. When she ventured out to sweep the porch and sidewalk, her neighbor, a fortune-teller, rushed out and greeted her with a hug and said, "Granny, I haven't seen you out for a few days. Have you been ill?"

"Yes, I haven't been too well lately," Granny replied. "I still haven't gone home to heaven yet, but I'm on my way."

The fortune-teller said, "Granny, I'm going to heaven with you."

My granny's reply was, "But, Honey, you've got to have a ticket to get into the city that I'm talking about."

How about you? Do you have your ticket?

ANN BURNEM
Ashland, Ky.
Song Evangelist

9

*Paul, an apostle of Jesus Christ by the will of God,
to the saints which are at Ephesus, and
to the faithful in Christ Jesus.*
(EPH. 1:1)

Saints Around the World

Saints in Ephesus? Incredible! Impossible! For Ephesus was widely known as the very center of idolatry, of sensual living, the home of the infamous shrine of Diana.

But in that very city there were saints. Real flesh-and-blood people reproducing the spirit and character of Jesus.

And I expect there are saints where you live, in the 1990s. For there are saints all over the world.

A missionary in India telling the story of Jesus was interrupted by a lad whose attention was caught by the charm of the old, old story and blurted out, "I know Him! I know Him! He lives near us." Saints in India too!

And there was the boy whose experience with saints was limited to the stained-glass windows at his church. So for him "saints are people that the light shines through."

Saints in Ephesus? Saints in India? Saints around the world!

LLOYD B. BYRON
Yukon, Okla.
Minister

Walking in the fear of the Lord, and in the comfort
of the Holy Ghost.
(ACTS 9:31)

Comforted in the Storm

I asked my students in a creative writing class to share an experience of finding comfort in circumstances that were threatening. One student gave the following incident.

"As a small child I was playing alone in my upstairs room when a summer storm suddenly swooped down and enveloped our house in whirling, solid sheets of rain. How the wind shrieked! Although it was only midafternoon, the sun was shrouded and darkness had come. The whole yard seemed to explode and blaze with angry lightning that was accompanied by unremitting, crashing thunder.

"I was terrified. I could neither run nor cry out. I froze in my little chair. Then comfort came. Mother called my name. I felt her gentle touch on my shoulder. The sound of her voice and the touch of her hand banished my fear."

What a high attainment to be able to live each hour of every day trusting the Father to take care of not only the small, fretful problems but also the times of darkness and storms. Let the responsibility of comfort in all of life's storms rest on Him. Trust God!

LEON CHAMBERS
Magnolia, Miss.
Minister, Teacher

They that wait upon the Lord shall renew their strength;
they shall mount up with wings as eagles; they shall run
and not be weary; and they shall walk, and not faint.

(ISA. 40:31)

Keep Walking!

For those of us who are older adults, walking is said to be the best exercise. Little children try to fly, young men and women engage in running marathons, but we just settle for walking—even a slow walk sometimes!

In the Meadowbrook subdivision where I live, I have a four-mile stretch that takes about an hour for me to walk. When I'm away from home, I explore the neighborhood for an hour or so as I try to keep up my exercise routine. Some friends my age get their walking in each morning at a nearby shopping mall before the stores open for business.

No question about it—walking is a good exercise; but walking with the Lord is even better! Paul urged young Timothy: "Exercise thyself . . . unto godliness" (1 Tim. 4:7). In these days of our lives when we don't have the strength to "spread our wings" and fly, or even to run, we can settle for an enjoyable walk with our Lord and renew our strength daily. This kind of walking can be done in a wheelchair or even in a hospital bed!

REEFORD L. CHANEY
Richmond, Va.
Pastor, District Superintendent, Evangelist

Be at peace with all men, if possible, so far as that depends on you.
(ROM. 12:18, Moffatt)

Living in Harmony

Two old men were having a discussion on the front porch of a retirement center. One of them was doing most of the talking and was quite animated as he presented his point of view. The other was sitting patiently waiting for an opening to give his side of the argument, glancing occasionally at the other old gentleman. A bystander was marveling at the patience of the old man, and then suddenly he realized that the man had his hearing aid turned off.

From time immemorial one of life's most frustrating problems has been that of living in harmony with one another. The problem arises from the fact that we are all endowed with a human nature, and Divine Providence has made us all different with varying points of view.

There are times when, in the interest of harmony, we must remain silent and forgo presenting our point of view. In his letter to the Romans, Paul points out that harmony is a personal responsibility: "Be at peace . . . so far as that depends on you."

DOYLE E. CLAY
Mount Vernon, Ohio
Minister

13

Dear friends, let us love one another, for love comes from God. Everyone who loves has been born of God and knows God. Whoever does not love does not know God, because God is love. This is how God showed his love among us: He sent his one and only Son into the world that we might live through him. This is love: not that we loved God, but that he loved us and sent his Son as an atoning sacrifice for our sins. Dear friends, since God so loved us, we also ought to love one another.

(1 JOHN 4:7-11, NIV)

Everlasting Mercy

He was old, and his long white beard glistened in the sunlight as he sat on the porch. Stopping to visit, I perceived his mind was totally gone. He talked incoherently. Kneeling by his rocking chair, I prayed that somehow this 93-year-old man could find Christ as his Savior.

One morning, after 14 years of insanity, my friend arose with a clear mind and wanted someone to pray with him. I was called, and the way of salvation was presented. Tears flowed into his beard as he confessed his sins to God. Those tears looked like diamonds as the smile and joy of sins forgiven covered his countenance. The day of victory ended, and upon arising the next morning, his mind was gone once more. In a few days he went to be with the Lord. My funeral text, "God is love," told of the depths of divine love in giving this old man 24 hours of sanity, after 14 years of insanity, so that he could find peace with his Maker. How great is the love of God to us!

M. E. CLAY
St. Marys, Ohio
District Superintendent

Submit yourselves therefore to God. Resist the devil, and he will flee from you. Draw nigh to God, and he will draw nigh to you. Cleanse your hands, ye sinners; and purify your hearts, ye double minded.

(JAMES 4:7-8)

Keep in Tune

Nothing irritates me more than a piano or violin out of tune. No matter how great the composition or the skill of the performer may be, if his instrument is out of tune, the performance is disappointing.

I indulged in one of my favorite pastimes recently by attending a great symphony concert. Before the performance, one violinist stood, sounded the A string, and waited until every instrument in that great orchestra was in tune with him. This was repeated at the beginning of the second half, making sure every instrument was in tune with the piano, which was played by a great pianist.

How much more important is it to have our souls and lives in tune with the teachings of Christ, His example, and the leading of the Holy Spirit. To be effective Christians and soul winners, to be assured of a home in heaven, demands we keep in tune with our Lord and Savior Jesus Christ. What blessed harmony this is.

JAMES V. COOK
Fostoria, Ohio
Minister of Music, Song Evangelist

15

For I am already being poured out like a drink offering, and the time has come for my departure. I have fought the good fight, I have finished the race, I have kept the faith.

(2 TIM. 4:6-7, NIV)

He Died on a Tree

Commitment to Christ does not expire with retirement. It is for life.

When the 1844 Conference voted to divide over slavery, Methodist clergyman Anthony Bewley declared allegiance to neither North nor South but to The Methodist Episcopal Church, U.S.A.!

Appointed to missions in 1858, Bewley moved his wife and six children to Texas, then slave territory. Urged not to return for a second term because of the bitter opposition given Northerners, Bewley replied, "Let them hang or burn me if they choose; hundreds will rise up out of my ashes."

Back in Texas, vigilante rule prevailed. When forced to flee, a $1,000 reward was offered for Bewley's capture. He was caught, and without trial, hung to die on a limb of a Fort Worth pecan tree. A farewell letter to family affirms both Bewley's innocence and his commitment to Christ.

Anthony Bewley, my great-grandfather, was no abolitionist but a man committed to God—my model of commitment and faithfulness. I am one of the "hundreds" to rise from his ashes, having preached 53 years.

EARL C. DARDEN
Nampa, Idaho
Pastor

For this reason, ever since I heard about your faith in the Lord Jesus and your love for all the saints, I have not stopped giving thanks for you, remembering you in my prayers.
(EPH. 1:15-16, NIV)

From Pity to Praise

Recently I was enjoying a pity party, feeling sorry for myself and getting lower by the hour.

The phone rang and a friend said, "Pastor, I just read Eph. 1:15-22 and can hardly contain the joy in my heart."

Upon reading the Word he described, my self-pity turned to victory. Paul prayed "that the God of our Lord Jesus Christ . . . may give you the Spirit of wisdom and revelation, so that you may know him better. . . . that the eyes of your heart may be enlightened in order that you may know the hope . . . and his incomparably great power. . . . That power is like . . . he exerted in Christ when he raised him from the dead" (vv. 17-20, NIV).

Glory!

By then I had forgotten my puny little selfish petitions and was rejoicing in the Lord.

Let me suggest we turn from our little thoughts to God's big ones. Why not read Paul's prayer to the Ephesians until it becomes part of us?

Aren't you glad we have such a great God?

HAROLD C. DAVIS
Choctaw, Okla.
Pastor

17

*O Lord, remember now how I have walked before
thee in truth and with a perfect heart, and have
done that which is good in thy sight.*

(2 KINGS 20:3)

Lord, I Am Glad

The phone rang. It was 8 A.M., Friday, August 20, 1981.
"Brother Drye, we have plenty of apples, two trees full;
come over and pick all you want," the party said. I left
home at 1 P.M. and went by a friend's house and bor-
rowed a 30-foot ladder. By 1:30 I was in the top of the
apple tree, 20 feet from the ground, picking the delicious,
ripened apples.

Just when my pouch was filling, the ladder slipped,
and I fell to the ground. I was knocked unconscious for a
moment, and everything turned red before my eyes. I
thought that I was dying. I later learned that my neck
had been broken. As I lay there, I could not move. I said,
"Lord, I am glad I don't have to ask You to forgive me of
anything. I am ready to go."

The rescue squad arrived, and I was taken to the
hospital, where I stayed 21 days. A steel halo was placed
on my head, and a full cast was placed on my body. I was
out of the pastorate four months. *"Lord, I am glad* my
body was not paralyzed." I am well and in the full-time
service of the King. *"Lord, I am glad* this was an incident
and not an accident in my life." God
has used it for the advancement of
His work.

J. T. DRYE
Kannapolis, N.C.
Pastor, Evangelist

18

Blessed are the peacemakers, for they will be called sons of God.
(MATT. 5:9, NIV)

Promoters of Praise

James says in his Epistle: "But the wisdom that comes from heaven is first of all pure; then peace-loving" (3:17, NIV)—the same order as here. If we are pure in heart—not wanting our own will, but only God's will—we will be helping to create peace around us, not strife and turmoil.

Are we really "peacemakers"? In our country, in our community? You say, "Yes." But how about in your church? One of the great tragedies of our day is a spirit of divisiveness in churches.

Dare we ask another question: "Are you a peacemaker in your home?" That is the most important place today!

Jesus said that peacemakers "will be called sons of God." This is the correct translation. When the definite article is omitted in Greek (as here), it emphasizes character. And when people make peace, they will be called "God's sons" because they act like God. In Eastern thinking "son of" means "having the nature of." If we claim to be Christians, let's act like it.

RALPH EARLE
Kansas City
Seminary Professor, Preacher, Teacher, Writer

Love one another.
(JOHN 13:34)

The Ministry of Encouragement

When Paul, so recently converted, arrived at Jerusalem, the church was afraid of him, remembering how he terrorized the Christians. But Barnabas embraced him as a brother and welcomed him (Acts 9).

Later when Mark was not considered dependable, Barnabas became his supporter in missionary coservice (Acts 15).

This writer has been blessed by some who had the same spirit as Barnabas, sometimes called the Son of Consolation. During my final semester of graduate work in Pasadena College, Prof. C. B. Widmeyer asked me if I had a call to a church. Finding that I did not, he said, "Today I will write some superintendents, recommending you." This led to an open door of 50 years spent in the ministry. Lots of "discouragers" have been forgotten, but the cherished memories of the "encouragers" like Barnabas remain vivid. The prayer of Francis of Assisi does seem so appropriate today: "Lord, grant that I may not so much seek to be consoled, as to console; to be loved, as to love . . ."

FRED F. FIKE
Amarillo, Tex.
Pastor, District Associate

20

I may do anything, but everything is not constructive.
(1 COR. 10:23, Phillips)

Stewardship of Life Never Ends!

Have you ever given serious thought to just taking it easy from now on? Before you really do that, think again! Where does Scripture give us permission to end our stewardship of life? Do I still have a personal obligation to positive involvement with my family, with other people, with personal improvement, with the church?

Now you already know the answers to these questions, but maybe you have never really reflected on them. Responsibilities may change drastically, but they never go away. We all know that total inactivity is death, and we surely don't want to move in that direction. Nor, on the other hand, do we want to develop a guilt trip that leads us into a state of feverish activity and sense of pressure. We've had enough of that! So what we really need is to open exciting doors into life and fulfillment and an ever-increasing sense of self-worth. And that can happen—for you.

We may not be able to control outward circumstances, but we can control what goes on inside. We can continue to develop the inner man, so that our lives become increasingly rich and rewarding as we actively take over our life and become real stewards of what we have left.

LYLE FLINNER
Bethany, Okla.
College Professor, Minister

21

I love the Lord, because he hath heard my voice and my supplications. Because he hath inclined his ear unto me, therefore will I call upon him as long as I live.

(PS. 116:1-2)

I Love the Lord

"I love the Lord." What a beautiful testimony! Hundreds of times it has been voiced by faithful Christians in Wednesday evening prayer meetings.

But why do we love the Lord? The Psalmist gave his reasons. Because the Lord had heard his voice, had heard his supplication, and had inclined His ear unto him.

What assurance! Like the Psalmist, we, too, have a Lord who listens. He can hear our *voices* —whether songs of praise, whispered prayers, or "groanings" of "the Spirit" (Rom. 8:26). He will listen to our *supplications,* our pleas for help, our cries for deliverance. With an "inclined . . . ear" He listens intently with undivided attention to our prayers.

Why do I love the Lord? Because He hears. Because He understands my words and my motives. Because He cares! Because He is able! I love Him because of who He is and what He has done, is doing, and will do. Most of all, "We love him, because he first loved us" (1 John 4:19).

He is listening! Call upon Him! Now!

JONATHAN T. GASSETT
Gainesville, Fla.
Pastor, District Superintendent

Nay, in all these things we are more than conquerors through him.
(ROM. 8:37)

A Niagara of Love

This passage comes from the pen of the great apostle after many years of experience. Lying in the background is that incident on the road to Damascus, as well as many other happenings in places like Philippi, Corinth, and Jerusalem.

Paul is rejoicing in the truth that has come to him in his walk with Christ. He knows only too well how vulnerable Christians are in living out their faith in a fallen world. But the more he writes, the more his confidence grows, until he can hold back no longer, and he cries, "Who [or what] shall separate us from the love of Christ? shall tribulation, or distress, . . . ?" (v. 35). Then he answers with a shout, "Nay, in all these things we are more than conquerors!"

As he writes, I seem to see his face take on a glow of divine radiance, and his words are touched with holy fire. He cannot stop with the above, for his words come pouring forth in a rushing stream that rises to a climax in a thundering crescendo of inspired truth: "For I am persuaded, that neither death, nor life, nor angels, nor principalities, nor powers . . . shall be able to separate us from the love of God, which is in Christ Jesus our Lord" (vv. 38-39).

What a torrent! What a Niagara of truth! A veritable "Hallelujah Chorus" on the love of God!

C. PAUL GRAY
Bethany, Okla.
Minister, Educator

23

Not that I . . . am already perfected . . . but one thing
I do, forgetting the things that are behind . . . I press
toward the goal . . . Let us therefore, as many as
are perfect, be thus minded.

(PHIL. 3:12-15, John Wesley's trans.)

Christians in the Making

"Perfect," but not "already perfected." This is the tension in which we live between Pentecost and the Parousia. We are "Christians in the making" (E. Stanley Jones).

Thank God we can be "perfect"—pure in heart. "Purity of heart is to will one thing" (Kierkegaard). By sanctifying grace we can say with Paul, "This *one* thing I do." To be evangelically perfect is not to be faultless but "attuned to our redeemed destiny in Christ."

But we are not yet "perfected." God is not finished with us. "There is a difference between one that is *perfect* and one that is *perfected*. The one is fitted for the race; the other, ready to receive the prize" (Wesley).

I'm a person God is making,
Like a statue God is shaping;
God is changing me, correcting—
God's intent on my perfecting.

I am not yet perfected—by a long shot! But I am "persuaded of this very thing, that he who hath begun a good work in [me] will perfect it until the day of Jesus Christ" (Phil. 1:6, Wesley).

WILLIAM M. GREATHOUSE
Mount Juliet, Tenn.
General Superintendent

He himself knew what he would do.
(JOHN 6:6)

Trusting in God

God does not panic, He need not; for He knows what He can and will do. When Israel stood before the Red Sea, pursued by Egypt's armies, the Lord said, "Fear ye not, stand still, and see the salvation of the Lord" (Exod. 14:13).

Word came that Jesus' friend Lazarus was sick; that message did not alarm Him, but He tarried, explaining to the disciples: "This sickness is not unto death, but for the glory of God, that the Son of God might be glorified thereby" (John 11:4).

There is a fascinating view of the Yosemite Valley as one exits from the Wawona Tunnel. The Lord's tunnels are a means of getting us to new revelations. Healing His friend Lazarus would help the family, but much more lasting comfort and hope would come from "I am the resurrection, and the life" (John 11:25).

He is God; He is more than able to succeed, and He will accomplish what is best. If one will wait and trust in Him, he can "know that I am the Lord: for they shall not be ashamed that wait for me" (Isa. 49:23).

HAROLD C. HARCOURT
Norman, Okla.
Pastor

The Lord is my shepherd; I shall not want.
(PS. 23:1)

*My God shall supply all your need according to his riches
in glory by Christ Jesus.*
(PHIL. 4:19)

Waiting on God

Few people would question the great resources of God. We know that His storehouses are full and overflowing and that He is able to supply our every need. Sometimes, however, when the answer to a particular prayer is delayed—not timed according to our schedule—we are apt to become anxious and even speculate on ways that the answer should come. At this juncture there is danger of mistaking our will for that of the will of God, even contriving ways that would seem to be the logical pattern for God to use in providing an answer to our petition. "Thy will be done" (Matt. 26:42) is always appropriate and a vital element in supplication. Whatever the circumstances, when the answer becomes reality, we recognize in it the divine handiwork—God working for our good and His glory.

> *God knows my need and all He will supply;*
> *I shall not want beneath His watchful eye.*
> *He knows the prayer I'm breathing constantly.*
> *God knows, and that's enough for me.**
>
> —FLOYD W. HAWKINS

*Copyright 1944.
Renewed 1972 by Lillenas Publishing Co.

FLOYD W. HAWKINS
Gladstone, Mo.
Elder, Music Editor

And it shall come to pass, that before they call, I will answer;
and while they are yet speaking, I will hear.

(ISA. 65:24)

No Trivial Petitions

My granddaughter called me "Oompa." When we and her parents talked on the telephone, there was always a treat at the end because Lynette would be tugging at them to let her talk before we hung up. It was always the same: "Oompa, do you know what?"

Then I would answer, "No, what?"

It was never the same twice, but more often than not it was some trivial thing that she thought of at the moment and proceeded to tell me all about it.

Don't think for a moment that it was anything but pure joy for me. I listened to every word and commented with enthusiasm. She was my granddaughter, and I was her "Oompa."

It gives me a great deal of satisfaction to feel that my Heavenly Father listens to me just like that. I come with my faltering, and not always logical, requests. He listens. He lets me know that I'm important to Him.

In a world of hurry and wait, when I'm a number to so many, it's good to know that I have a standing invitation to call on Him. He's never too busy. Any time of the day or night, I can ring in, "Jesus, do You know what?"

RAY J. HAWKINS
Pueblo, Colo.
Pastor, Senior Adult and Children's Worker

27

The simplicity that is in Christ.
(2 COR. 11:3)

Simple Gifts

There is much in this world that I do not understand. I am glad for people who are intellectually brilliant. Some folks are gifted with IQs and can explore all the deep mysteries of the universe. There are others who can take these findings and translate them into easier terms. We are all richer because of them.

I am glad, however, that most of the gifts of God are very simple. The gospel message is very plain and clear. It is the fact that Christ died for us and if, by faith, we accept His atoning benefits, we are saved. There is nothing complicated about that. Our day-by-day relationship with God does not require any gigantic feat, nor does it require intellectual superiority. Even the person with limited intelligence can understand what it means to know the Lord as Savior and to live daily with a sense of His presence. Let us this day realize that the simplicity that the apostle Paul saw in Christ and wrote about to the Corinthian church reaches out to us for our spiritual welfare.

ROSS W. HAYSLIP
Tucson, Ariz.
Pastor

28

Let not your heart be troubled: ye believe in God, believe also in me. In my Father's house are many mansions: if it were not so, I would have told you. I go to prepare a place for you.
(JOHN 14:1-2)

An Untroubled Heart

My wife and I were visiting one of our Prime Timers in a local hospital. I included the lady in the next bed in my prayer. As we were leaving, she thanked me for the prayer. Ara Hooser appeared to be in her 80s, her body twisted and frail. She began quoting a poem of her own composition. It spoke of the beauties of life and nature and then compared it with the joys and blessings we shall enjoy in the "place He is preparing" for His own. She was a widow of 16 years who lived alone and maintained her own house, though she was almost blind.

My wife, Martha, suggested that we sing for her before leaving. So we sang "Until Then," and Ara Hooser clapped her tired hands, rejoicing in the words "with joy I'll carry on."

We had gone to cheer others but left brightened by the "ray of sunshine"—little Mrs. Hooser.

H. HARVEY HENDERSHOT
Nashville
Pastor, District Superintendent

For the preaching of the cross is to them that perish foolishness; but unto us which are saved it is the power of God.
(1 COR. 1:18)

Begin at the Cross

Tommy Elliott was raised in London near Charing Cross Station. Tommy played in the streets since there were no backyards or parks. One day as Tommy ran and played with his friends in the streets, he found himself in unfamiliar territory. He was lost! A London bobby (policeman) found him sitting on the street, crying. Tommy could give his name to the policeman but could not give him his home address. When the policeman inquired about the area where Tommy lived, he quickly responded by saying, "Sir, if you will take me to the cross, I can find my way home from there."

Tommy's statement speaks for all of us. People all around us are lost and cannot find their way. If you and I will get them to the Cross, they will find their way home! The hymn writer Sir John Bowring said it best when he wrote, "In the cross of Christ I glory." Life takes a new turn and we are able to find our way in life when we meet Jesus at the Cross.

THOMAS HERMON
Winter Haven, Fla.
Pastor, District Superintendent

Likewise the Spirit also helpeth our infirmities.
(ROM. 8:26)

For we have not an high priest which cannot be touched with the feeling of our infirmities.
(HEB. 4:15)

In Our Weakness

A most important happening occurred in the Early Church on the Day of Pentecost. However, the work of the blessed Holy Spirit can be seen in both the Old and the New Testaments. In our day let us not overlook one of His important functions as recorded in Rom. 8:26. Here we are told: "Likewise the Spirit also helpeth our infirmities." The dictionary tells us that an infirmity is a physical weakness or ailment (the infirmities of age). To help us means that the Holy Spirit takes hold of our infirmities, together with us on the other side. He lifts with us. He does not expect us to carry our infirmities alone. He makes intercession to the Father for us.

Also in Heb. 4:15 we are told that Christ, our Great High Priest, is "touched with the feeling of our infirmities." Jesus knows just how we feel, and His great heart of love is touched.

In the light of the above let us say with the apostle Paul: "Most gladly therefore will I rather glory in my infirmities, that the power of Christ may rest upon me" (2 Cor. 12:9).

PAUL H. HETRICK, SR.
Temple City, Calif.
Missionary

For what is your life?
(JAMES 4:14)

More than a Vapor

James says life is a vapor that appears for a little while. But life is more than a brief existence.

First, life is a field for unselfish service. Note I said unselfish service. Some people perform religious acts for their own benefit and gain. Jesus said, "Many will say to me in that day, Lord, Lord, have we not prophesied in thy name? and in thy name have cast out devils? and in thy name done many wonderful works? And then will I profess unto them, I never knew you: depart from me, ye that work iniquity" (Matt. 7:22-23).

Second, life is a crucible for molding character. Reputation is man's exterior, character is man's interior. The process is something like the following: Sow a thought, reap an act. Sow an act, reap a habit. Sow a habit, reap a character. Sow a character, reap a destiny. Character is the only thing that will cross the divide of worlds with us, so be sure and mold it well.

Third, life is a prelude to an everlasting existence, like some musical compositions that have what is known as a prelude (only a few bars, then the main body of the song). The song is much longer than the prelude. So the present life is a few brief moments compared to the life eternal.

CHARLES A. HIGGINS
Las Cruces, N.Mex.
Minister

But the path of the righteous is like the light of dawn,
that shines brighter and brighter until the full day.
(PROV. 4:18, NASB)

Our Bright Hope

Never shall I forget seeing my first sunrise while flying east over the Atlantic. There was a deep darkness just before dawn. Then one streak of black paled into gray. As the gray blanket inched across the eastern sky, it increasingly paled, and objects took on a shadowy image—the wings and motors of the plane became a shadowy outline against the sky.

The gray became silver and a glimmer of light burst into scores of splinters as they melted into a patch of light and quickly chased the gray and silver over the horizon. With steady insistence each shadow was chased out of the deepest corners, and the whole east was light.

This was followed by one streak of red, then 2, 6, 20—100 streaks. Slowly they crawled back into the red ball that was creeping over the horizon. In a blaze of glory the sunlight burst forth—and it was day!

How directly this is in conflict with the common cycle of life and death all around us—beginning, growing, climaxing, declining. Thank God, that is not His plan for us! But it doesn't "just happen"! We have a vital responsibility! The holy life consists not only of a crisis but the pursuit of the *goal*—being conformed to His image. We don't need to grow old listless, dependent, hopeless, despairing. We can live with a bright hope. He would unfold and enlarge us until that glorious day—a sunrise for us, not a sunset. One dear lady who lived with that radiance shared with me her secret. "I want to grow old, not just gracefully but usefully." May God help us!

DICK HOWARD
Bethany, Okla.
Pastor, Professor, Evangelist

33

And whoever in the name of a disciple gives to one of these little ones even a cup of cold water to drink, truly I say to you he shall not lose his reward.

(MATT. 10:42, NASB)

A Call to Ministry

Have you ever said to yourself, "Here I am, retired. There's not much, if anything, I can do for the Lord"?

You have no doubt heard about Mother Teresa, the long-past-retirement-age sister in India. She sees Jesus in everyone she serves.

This concept makes the most lowly task she performs a gift to Him, no matter the repulsiveness of what she might be doing for a sick or dying soul.

Most of us aren't being asked to follow in Mother Teresa's footsteps, but there are many who need "just a cup of cold water" (Beck) in Jesus' name. What *is* a cup of cold water? It could be just a phone call to someone you missed last Sunday in your Sunday School class or in the church service. Or it could be a card or note to someone who is ill and shut in. Some of us can fix a tasty casserole and take it to that one who just returned home, on shaky legs, from the hospital. Or no doubt there is a shut-in you might visit. Can't we all give a cup of cold water to someone?

WINI HOWARD
Bethany, Okla.
Housewife, Teacher

For I acknowledge my transgressions: and my sin is ever before me. . . . Purge me with hyssop, and I shall be clean: wash me, and I shall be whiter than snow. . . . Create in me a clean heart, O God.

(PS. 51:3, 7, 10)

An Intense Desire

The temperature has hovered between 20 and 30 degrees for the past two days, while a cold rain has been falling. I saw two blue jays fluttering and flapping as only they can, taking a bath in that cold water at the front of my driveway. Brrh! What an intense desire for cleanliness!

There is a continuing, agonizing desire in the soul sensitized by the life of the Spirit to be free from the loathsome, defiling presence of the sin that remains in the justified heart. The prayer of David to God was "Purge me . . . and I shall be clean: wash me . . . Create in me a clean heart." Mildred Cope sang, "Make me clean; oh, make me pure! / I must know the double cure!"* Such a prayer finds its answer in the cleansing work of the Holy Spirit. That cleansed soul is at the same time filled with the loving presence of the abiding Comforter.

"Bathe my soul in Thy loving fullness, O Lord!"

J. LEWIS INGLE
Carrollton, Tex.
Minister

*God is our refuge and strength, an ever-present help in trouble.
Therefore we will not fear, though the earth give way
and the mountains fall into the heart of the sea,
though its waters roar and foam and the
mountains quake with their surging.* Selah.

(PS. 46:1-3, NIV)

God Is Our Refuge

Man faces life that is complicated with distress, confusion, frustration, and despair. There is a God with power, strength, and wisdom who is in charge, ready to help.

We see a personal God. The omnipotent, eternal, Creator God is my personal God. He is a caring God who is a personal companion in life's situations. "The Lord is my shepherd" (Ps. 23:1).

He is a protecting God; He is our Refuge. "He that dwelleth in the secret place of the most High shall abide under the shadow of the Almighty. . . . He shall cover thee with his feathers, and under his wings shalt thou trust," secured from the storms and calamities of life (Ps. 91:1, 4).

He is a providing God; He is our Strength and present Help. "He giveth power to the faint; and to them that have no might he increaseth strength" (Isa. 40:29). God is the great Giver of life, love, salvation, health, and life's necessities.

God gives us a victorious, full, and meaningful life.

R. A. ISBELL
Baton Rouge, La.
Pastor, Evangelist

Jesus saith unto her, Touch me not; for I am not yet ascended
to my Father: but go to my brethren, and say unto them,
I ascend unto my Father, and your Father;
and to my God, and your God.

(JOHN 20:17)

No Permanent Home

Christ's ascension is comforting and edifying to every child of God. It assures us of the certainty of our redemption. It also reminds the believer that we have no continuing city here but seek one to come. Neither the godly nor the wicked abide permanently on this earth. The godly look for better things; the wicked, though they desire to remain, cannot stay.

The Christian reminds himself that the time will come when he will leave his house, clothes, possessions, and dear ones. But the Christian believes that when the struggle ends here, he will ascend into heaven to a place awaiting him in glory. Thus as Christians we cease to love the world, and we cling to Christ in faith. We forsake the world by no longer living according to its will and customs, but rather living according to the will of God.

Therefore, when we think of heaven, we can say to ourselves, "Yonder is my homeland, my heritage, and my future eternal home."

ORVILLE W. JENKINS
Leawood, Kans.
General Superintendent

Because Christ also suffered for us, leaving us an example,
that ye should follow his steps.
(1 PET. 2:21)

My Daily Prayer

Our daily prayer should be to become more like Jesus each day of our life. Think of the character of Christ, and then pray, *Lord, help me to be more like You in these areas of my life:*

Like Christ in love. He loved us so much that He gave His life for us.

Like Christ in prayer. He often spent entire nights in prayer.

Like Him in giving. "The good shepherd giveth his life for the sheep" (John 10:11).

Like Him in holiness. "Be ye holy; for I am holy" (1 Pet. 1:16).

Like Him in obedience. "I do always those things that please [the Father]" (John 8:29).

Like Him in humility. He washed the feet of His disciples.

Like Christ in our willingness to suffer if need be. "Christ also suffered for us" (1 Pet. 2:21).

Like Him in compassion. "He was moved with compassion" (Matt. 9:36).

Like Christ in forgiveness. "Forgive them; for they know not what they do" (Luke 23:34).

LEON JENNINGS
Bethany, Okla.
Pastor

38

"How did this man get such learning without having studied?" Jesus answered, "My teaching is not my own. It comes from him who sent me."

(JOHN 7:15-16, NIV)

"With God . . ."

Our world fell apart. Unknown to me or my doctors, cancer was permeating my body. This was a result of misdiagnosis, which we had misread for years. In November 1989 the verdict was "You have till Christmas." But God asked in answer to prayer, "Which Christmas?" Nausea, chemotherapy, radiation.

I said, like the apostle Paul, "I am . . . betwixt two" things (Phil. 1:23). My sweetheart of 50 years encouraged me to fight. In the hospital, dying, they weighed me. "Why?" I asked. Afterward I mused, "They must be figuring how many pallbearers they need."

Jesus said, "Everything is possible for him who has faith!" (Mark 9:23, Williams). Our Christmas was the best. It is February, and strength, appetite, and limbs are responding. How much time remains to finish the tasks my Father and Savior, Jesus Christ, allows is with Him.

I have much to say to this day's generation about Jesus, who still says, "Come, repent, and sin no more. I am with you. The truth [I am He] will set and keep you free." The essence of living for us—His truth: "Without me ye can do nothing" (see John 8:10-12, 32, 36; 15:5).

MATHEW R. KORODY (deceased)
Kansas City
Pastor, Missionary, Evangelist

For he himself is our peace, who has made the two one and has destroyed the barrier, the dividing wall of hostility, by abolishing in his flesh the law with its commandments and regulations. His purpose was to create in himself one new man out of the two, thus making peace.

(EPH. 2:14-15, NIV)

A Piece of History

On December 4, 1989, two young friends of ours were at the Berlin Wall. They saw it coming down in pieces. We saw it with the rest of the world via television, and how moved we were with emotion. We had lived through the erection of this wall, built in hatred and fear, bringing division. Our friends brought us an unusual and actual piece of the wall and placed it on a card with the title "A Piece of History." This is displayed before me on my desk.

Well! "A Piece of History"—of course. Yet my heart was blessed as I changed that phrase to say, "The Peace of History." Now there is no wall, only a bridge and not a drawbridge. Jesus Christ, our Lord, on the Cross has torn down "the middle wall of partition" (v. 14) and has granted us peace, thus making us one. Jesus has called to every person everywhere, "Peace."

EARL G. LEE
Wrightwood, Calif.
Pastor, Missionary

*And Jacob said . . . , The days of the years of my pilgrimage
are an hundred and thirty years.*

(GEN. 47:9)

Our Pilgrimage

Thus Jacob replied to Pharaoh. I like the way he answered, for it reveals his concept of life here on earth. To him life was a journey. He had not considered this earth as his abode, nor his destiny.

Life is a pilgrimage. The dictionary defines pilgrimage as a journey with an objective. Life for Jacob was traveling toward the final meeting with the God of Abraham, his God—Jehovah—through eternity.

Such a concept of life is essential to every Christian. It is necessary to keep the transitory things of this world in proper perspective. It is the reference point from which we Christians make basic decisions and measure the issues of life. It is the road we travel, straight and true across the years. It is the challenge that calls us onward to better things in the Lord. It keeps us alert, for travel requires attention to the road. It brings new scenes and vistas for our enjoyment. The destiny is worthwhile and the pilgrimage is joyous. Let us travel on.

V. H. LEWIS
Olathe, Kans.
General Superintendent

41

*Whatever your hand finds to do, do it with all your might, for
in the grave, where you are going, there is neither working
nor planning nor knowledge nor wisdom.*
(ECCLES. 9:10, NIV)

Making a Difference

This is an exhortation from the wise man to present
activity—not what he did yesterday, not what he would
like to do tomorrow. An exhortation based on the fact
that a particular work is allotted to each life. "Whatever
your hand finds to do." We are urged to present activity
because opportunity once lost can never be regained.

Solomon's word stresses the importance of earnest-
ness. "Do it with all your might." If we would share
Christ's victory, we must share His sincerity.

This is a recommendation to faithfulness in dis-
charging our stewardship responsibility. We may not be
able to do as much as we formerly did, but we can do
something in God's kingdom.

While walking on a beach at an early hour, a youth
saw an elderly man picking up starfish and throwing
them into the ocean. The young man asked him why he
was doing that. He answered: "The stranded starfish will
die in the morning sun if left on the beach."

The youth responded, "This beach extends for hundreds of miles, and there are millions of starfish. How
can what you are doing make any difference?"

The old man immediately threw the starfish into the
sea and simply said, "It makes a difference to that one."

Our contribution in life may not be on the scale it
once was, but whatever our hands find to do is important. We will keep praying, witnessing, giving, loving—it
makes a difference to someone. "Oc-
cupy till I come."

W. RAYMOND McCLUNG
Nacogdoches, Tex.
**Pastor, District Superintendent,
College Professor**

Fear thou not; for I am with thee: be not dismayed; for I am thy God: I will strengthen thee; yea, I will help thee; yea, I will uphold thee with the right hand of my righteousness.
(ISA. 41:10)

For I the Lord thy God will hold thy right hand, saying unto thee, Fear not; I will help thee.
(ISA. 41:13)

The Secret of His Presence

A long time ago in the small town of Curtis, Nebr., Nazarene Evangelists M. F. Linard and Q. A. Deck came to our town, pitched a tent, and preached the gospel. Along with my parents, brothers, and sisters, I found Jesus at that altar, where I bowed my head and wept. Joy swept into my heart, and the Church of the Nazarene has been my church ever since.

I was a young child then, and many more times I've sought the Lord for forgiveness and divine direction. I remember when we moved to Santa Monica, Calif., where I battled with a serious heart condition. It was there that Jesus healed my heart.

During those days of illness I learned how great it was to have a friend like Jesus. He is closer than a brother, a friend we can trust, one who shares our problems, our hurts, our anxieties.

Later He called me to the ministry, and I've learned that whosoever shall do the will of His Father has a close relationship with Jesus.

Prayer is the secret place where we lay our deepest yearnings, weeping in sincerity for the lost. Seeking to know our Lord and His will costs time, strength, and obedience; but oh, what joy as we come to know Him in the secret of His presence.

DORIS M. McDOWELL
Sierra Madre, Calif.
Minister

I saw a new heaven . . . And I heard a loud voice . . . saying,
God will wipe away every tear from their eyes . . .
and there will be no more death . . . no more pain!
These former things have all passed away.

(REV. 21:4)

Pain—the Unwanted Guest!

Pain was no stranger to the man who had 13 major operations with constant, debilitating torment. His friends could not comprehend the never-ending hurt. It was as though pain had knocked at his door and said, "I have come to stay!"

The Ohio Pain and Stress Treatment Center indicates that Americans spend $70 million each year to be free from their ailments.

Pain humbles the proud, softens the stubborn, melts the hard, and silently wins the battle deep within the lonely soul. Pain seems to operate alone, without assistance; it communicates its own message and refuses to be ignored!

George Matheson prayed, "Dear God, have I ever thanked You for my thorns? I know I've thanked You a thousand times for my roses—but not once for my thorns. Teach me the glory of my cross; and show me by the path of pain that my tears have made my rainbow!"

Lift your eyes toward the city of God, and hear His voice say to you, "There shall be no more pain!"

ORVILLE L. MAISH
Toledo, Ohio
Minister

44

The lines are fallen unto me in pleasant places;
yea, I have a goodly heritage.

(PS. 16:6)

Our Ultimate Need

A warm, comforting sense of well-being accompanies God's children who have chosen to follow Christ, have tried to mold their lives and thoughts and actions to harmonize with His will, and have completed the active years.

We still ask: "What do I yet desire of life?" and our Lord answers, "Be thou faithful unto death"!

Fortunately for us, our "want list" shrinks dramatically with the passing days! After years of serving in the workplace, we attach more importance to a few basic needs and a simple life-style.

David spoke to our needs in this psalm (read it carefully). Note verse 7, "I will praise the Lord, who counsels me" (NIV). Verse 8, "Because He is at my right hand, I will not be shaken" (NIV). The climax is found in verses 9-11: "Therefore my heart is glad and my tongue rejoices; my body also will rest secure, because you will not abandon me . . . You have made known to me the path of life; you will fill me with joy in your presence" (NIV).

M. L. MANN
Prescott, Ariz.
District Superintendent

Father, I will that they also, whom thou hast given me, be with me where I am; that they may behold my glory.
(JOHN 17:24)

Just Another Step

Retirement is just another step in the will of God for the Christian. It need not be a feeble step of inactivity.

Living consists of a series of steps, beginning with the first one as a child to the final step of death. Although our steps are influenced by the environment of home, school, and such, we are not totally controlled by it.

Mother Teresa looked from her boarding room window and saw people existing in poverty and dying without dignity. The desperate plight of the poor and helpless prompted her to respond to the need. She left the comfort of an affluent assignment and stepped into a life of sacrificial servanthood ministry.

Missionary E. Stanley Jones suffered a severe stroke after a full life of vital ministry. His mind and dedication were not impaired. Painfully he struggled to overcome his physical handicap. His reaction to life under pressure and submission to God in suffering is an example to us. His book *A Divine Yes*, written through loving concern and with determination to share his faith in the middle of life's adversities, crowned an exemplary life.

Our lives may not have public recognition as those just mentioned. Nevertheless, our remaining steps can be meaningful and fulfilling.

Jesus prayed, "Father, I will that they . . . be with me where I am." Christ's prayer will be answered for the Christian to be with Him when the final step is taken.

MARK R. MOORE
Nairobi, Kenya
Minister, Educator, Missionary

Thy word have I hid in mine heart,
that I might not sin against thee.

(PS. 119:11)

Hiding His Word

The Psalmist's "declaration of dependence" upon God is enhanced by the testimony that the Word (truth) had been implanted into his very being in a way that would undergird him in times of pressures or duress. This strengthening is parallel to the promise of the Father to the faithful that His Spirit not only had been with them but now could and would, if invited, be in them and guide them in the way of all truth.

With this type of guidance one need not be overcome by the enemy, even though it could appear that one is overtaken by, caught up in, or surrounded by, sin. This undergirding strength causes a determined unyielding to sin. It is a distinct fulfillment of the prayer of our Master when He said, "I pray not that thou shouldest take them out of the world, but that thou shouldest keep them from the evil" (John 17:15). As we hide (establish) His Word in our heart, there is a transcending knowledge that we are not of this world and the witness that we are sanctified "through thy truth: thy word is truth" (John 17:17).

The Christian in today's fast-lane society is blessed with an inner strength that drives him to have compassion for the lost and attempt to, by some means, share this blessing with them. Let us be "into the Word" "that the world may know" (John 17:23).

MERRILL M. MORGAN
Fritch, Tex.
Minister

Moses answered the people, "Do not be afraid. Stand firm and you will see the deliverance the Lord will bring you today. . . . The Lord will fight for you; you need only to be still."

(EXOD. 14:13-14, NIV)

Stand Firm!

You have heard the saying "adding insult to injury." This is the way it was for the children of Israel. After 430 years of bitter bondage in Egypt coming to an end, God's chosen people were finally free—or were they?

Pharaoh changed his mind—again! Seeing the impossibility of crossing the Red Sea, the Israelites were ready to give up when they saw Pharaoh's best warriors bearing down on them.

At that moment of desperation, Moses said, "Stand firm . . . The Lord will fight for you; you need only to be still." And you know the rest of the story. The waters divided and God's people crossed safely while Pharaoh's army drowned.

No matter where you are today, God will fight your battles for you. Today may be your day to stand firm, hold steady, and see the glory of the Lord! Remember the hymn "Be Still, My Soul"? The writer states, "The Lord is on thy side"!

J. V. MORSCH
Orlando, Fla.
Pastor, District Superintendent

And it came to pass, that, as the people pressed upon him to hear the word of God, he stood by the lake of Gennesaret.
(LUKE 5:1)

Jesus said unto Simon, "Fear not; from henceforth thou shalt catch men."
(LUKE 5:10)

Jesus Speaks to Us Personally

In Luke 5:1-11 Jesus speaks to the multitudes; He also speaks to one individual. To Simon Peter He said, "Fear not; from henceforth thou shalt catch men."

In the embrace of divine concern we are never just another face in the crowd. Nicodemus discovered it so when Jesus said to him personally, "God so loved the world, that he gave his only begotten Son, that whosoever believeth in him should not perish, but have everlasting life" (John 3:16).

So when we open the Book of God, it is fitting indeed that we pray, "Lord, what do You have to say to me this day? 'Speak, Lord, for thy servant heareth'" (1 Sam. 3:9).

FORREST W. NASH
Olathe, Kans.
Pastor, District Superintendent

49

My grace is sufficient for you, for my power
is made perfect in weakness.
(2 COR. 12:9, NIV)

Grace Sufficient

The person that has found his place under the umbrella of grace has many reasons to rejoice and to be filled with praise. There is no other covering in life that gives so much in benefits.

The grace of our Lord Jesus Christ has brought about salvation for a sinner. John Newton expressed it in song: "That saved a wretch like me." The Psalmist recorded, "They cried to the Lord in their trouble, and he saved them from their distress" (107:13, NIV).

The grace of our Lord Jesus Christ becomes a supplier of protection from "dangers, toils, and snares." It is truly inconceivable that one on the journey of life can be insecure in the wonderful coverage that the Savior gives. J. Bruce Evans wrote, "His grace is enough for me, ... / Through sorrow and pain, / Through loss or gain, / His grace is enough for me."

The grace of our Lord Jesus Christ brings one into an eternal home. The Psalmist stated, "He guided them to their desired haven" (107:30, NIV). Heaven is man's desired haven. Jesus said, "In my Father's house are many rooms; if it were not so, I would have told you. I am going there to prepare a place for you. ... I will come back and take you to be with me that you also may be where I am" (John 14:2-3, NIV). Man praises Him! What more would a person need? Let everyone praise Him for his deeds and "for his wonderful works to the children of men!" (Ps. 107:8, 15, 21, 31).

CLIFTON NORELL
Oklahoma City
Minister

Are not all angels ministering spirits sent to serve those who will inherit salvation?

(HEB. 1:14, NIV)

An Angel Can Have Fur

On Saturday afternoon during the revival meeting, the evangelist suddenly became anxious about his family. But after a few minutes alone with God, he claimed the promise, "Cast thy burden upon the Lord, and he shall sustain thee" (Ps. 55:22). And He did!

After the meeting concluded on Sunday night, the preacher went home. Upon his arrival, he heard the story and saw the big, shaggy yellow dog that had come on Saturday afternoon and taken his place against the front door and refused to move.

About midnight there had been a noise at the back screen like a hook being lifted from its place. The dog had heard the noise and charged around the house, barking furiously. The sound of running feet indicated someone making a hasty retreat. God's angel, in fur, was sent to protect the family from an intruder. "The angel of the Lord encampeth round about them that fear him, and delivereth them" (Ps. 34:7).

Mission accomplished, the dog disappeared.

JOE NORTON
Hamlin, Tex.
Pastor, Evangelist

Redeeming the time, because the days are evil.
(EPH. 5:16)

Redeeming the Time

The J.O.Y. (Just Older Youth) group in our church successfully conducts activities for the elderly that help in their use of time. The importance of time and its use cannot be overestimated. It becomes either a monstrous master or a majestic minister.

To some, it presents many happy opportunities. To others, it becomes an unscrupulous master. Whether we shall master time or it shall master us depends upon our will and initiative.

Obviously time places a limitation on the actual minutes we can devote to God's service. God's time must come first. Our own concerns must be secondary.

Time can deprive us of the reality of religion by denying us moments of meditation with God.

But time can be transformed from a monstrous master to a majestic minister if first things are really *first* and we redeem the time in service given and love shown to others in His name.

L. S. OLIVER
Colorado Springs
Minister, College President

See, I have set before thee this day life.
(DEUT. 30:15)

Finding Happiness

On leaving a small town in Oklahoma, one notices an unusual sign. In bold letters is the message: "TURN BACK! You've missed it!" At the bottom of the sign is the name of a gourmet ham sandwich place.

Some people who search for happiness all their lives frequently come to the end of the way feeling they have missed it. They ask, "How did I miss it?" Someone who had reached the "golden summit years" once said, "Isn't there some magic formula by which we could get ahold of a sense of happiness and fulfillment from the fleeting days?" But happiness is a by-product. It seldom, if ever, comes when we seek it as an end in itself. There could be some signposts to help us. The poet Henry Van Dyke put it in these words:

> *Four things a man must learn to do*
> *If he would make his record true:*
> *To think without confusion clearly,*
> *To love his fellowman sincerely,*
> *To act from honest motives purely,*
> *To trust in God and heaven securely.*

WENDELL O. PARIS
Henryetta, Okla.
District Superintendent

53

Never will I leave you; never will I forsake you.
(HEB. 13:5, NIV)

Jesus Christ is the same yesterday and today and forever.
(HEB. 13:8, NIV)

Kaleidoscope

In the midst of an urban renewal project downtown stands a century-old building steeped in memories of the city's flamboyant past. By current architectural standards it is somewhat of a monstrosity, certainly out of place amid the sleek new buildings rising around it. Yet there are loud protests from the purists against its demolition. "Save this last remaining link with the classic past," they plead.

But change is the most certain characteristic of life. Indeed it seems to be taking place at an accelerated pace these days. Something new is always coming along to displace or replace what has been pushed into obsolescence. Durability has become a highly relative term. Fads, fashions, and fancies alter with every new breeze. We live in an unstable world in which everything from nations to notions combine in a kaleidoscope of change.

In the midst of this chaos, how reassuring to know that "God is still on the throne." He is unchanging; His love never fails; His power is unabated; and His mercy endures forever.

J. FRED PARKER
Prairie Village, Kans.
Book Editor, NPH

And the Lord said to Moses, "I will do the very thing you have asked, because I am pleased with you and I know you by name."
(EXOD. 33:17)

Tapping God's Resources

Many years ago I heard Dr. E. Stanley Jones conclude a chapel talk with a thought-provoking prayer. It went something like this: "Teach me how to tap the resources Thou hast put within awaiting my ability to call on them and use them. Amen."

It was Dr. Jones's strong feeling that God has placed resources at our disposal waiting to be used. Through the years I am sure that these resources have been used many times, but there are other resources waiting to be claimed. Could it be that I have not received because I have not asked?

An interesting story came out of a Japanese prison camp about the frail 105-pound woman who was able to carry her material goods that weighed over 200 pounds. Evidently there were physical resources available to her for the difficult task that she knew little about.

In the sunset years of life, I shall have new and varied needs. How reassuring it is to know that there are resources available to me that are waiting for me to tap and use. This very day I can be adequate with God's resources.

My prayer today:

"O God, assist me to tap all the resources You have for me, since You know my name and my needs, and give me the ability to use them profitably in the hours when I seem to run out of resources, be it in sickness or in health. Amen."

KENNETH PEARSALL
Nampa, Idaho
Pastor, District Superintendent, College President

*Praise the Lord. Give thanks to the Lord, for he is good;
his love endures forever.*

(PS. 106:1, NIV)

Your Love for Me Is Forever!

I don't know about you, but I must confess: I have questioned God's love for me—just for me.

When I dwell on my pain, my losses, my sickness, my financial trouble, soon I feel wretched and discouraged. My energy goes. Negatives take over. I'm ready to quit.

Have you ever felt this way? And when it's dark, I can't see the light.

What can you do when you feel depressed, discouraged, disheartened?

1. Make a positive statement—*aloud:*
   Your love for me is forever!
2. Write on a card and carry it with you:
   Your love for me is forever!
3. Read it aloud both morning and night:
   Your love for me is forever!

Choices are mine. My battle is in my thoughts and feelings. So I choose to think and meditate on the eternal. For what I see today will only be memory tomorrow. But what is eternal, His love and His presence, that is my security. He is my everlasting Love!

MILTON E. POOLE
Salem, Oreg.
Pastor, Counselor

Let us hold firmly to our faith.
(HEB. 4:14, Phillips)

Hold On, Son

This is a gray morning. My wife, now an invalid, is despondent, unrestful, nervous, and unhappy. She cannot control her emotions. This is not the Lois I have known through the years. Brain damage is causing all of this. I feel that I am barely holding on, inches from despair. I simply cannot continue to see her go on this way. "What shall I do, Lord?" I cry in my agony and frustration.

As I open the Bible, I cry, "O God, speak to me." My eyes fall on this verse: "Let us hold firmly to our faith" (Heb. 4:14, Phillips). The following verse says that Christ, our High Priest, knows all about our weaknesses and is able to deal sympathetically with us. I seem to hear Him say, "Son, I know what you are going through, for when I walked on earth, I went down the very same road. I know you are being tested almost to the breaking point, but hold on; stay in there. I am, even now, presenting your need to the Father."

"Thank You, Lord!"

LYLE K. POTTER
Pomona, Calif.
Minister

He has gone in to be the guest of a sinner!
(LUKE 19:7, Weymouth)

Jesus the Guest of Sinners

"Here Jesus shocked the sensibilities of the crowd by inviting himself to be the guest of this chief publican and notorious sinner who had robbed nearly everybody in the city by exorbitant taxes" (A. T. Robertson, *Word Pictures* 2:240). Zacchaeus was an unpopular fellow. He deserved his title but not the treatment of Jesus' critics. Does a man's character improve by rubbing his nose in the dirt? Is this a case of what Paul Sherer would call "God out of bounds"? (Cf. *Interpreter's Bible* 8:234.)

Do we not sing from our hymnals, "Let Jesus Come into Your Heart"? (*Worship in Song,* 229). Did not God come to such persons as Abraham the Liar, Jacob the Thief, Moses the Murderer, Rahab the Harlot, and David the Adulterer? Then why should Jesus overlook Zacchaeus? Somewhere between the limb of the sycamore tree and the ground Zacchaeus repented, for when his feet hit the grass, he promised a fourfold restitution to those he had defrauded. Jesus paused on the road to Calvary to lodge in the house of Zacchaeus and to declare, "This day is salvation come to this house" (v. 9).

As Lloyd C. Douglas has pictured it: " 'Zacchaeus,' said the Carpenter gently, 'What did you see that made you desire this peace?' 'Good Master . . . I saw . . . mirrored in your eyes . . . the face of the Zacchaeus I was meant to be.' " (Cf. his sermon "The Mirror," *The American Pulpit Series* [New York and Nashville: Abingdon Cokesbury, 1945], bk. 2, 74.)

ROSS E. PRICE
Colorado Springs
Pastor, Educator, Author, Evangelist,
District Superintendent

Now faith is the substance of things hoped for,
the evidence of things not seen. For by it the
elders obtained a good testimony.
(HEB. 11:1-2, NKJV)

Open Doors

The key to a "great day" is *faith*. It is not a term that we pluck from the heavens, but a response to the perfect and sufficient sacrifice of Jesus Christ. It is a trust that opens for us a door into the very presence of God, in whose presence we can come with holy boldness, free from all fear and confident of forgiveness in the face of God.

This word of encouragement is found in both definitive and descriptive language. Faith is the "substance of things hoped for"—a concrete reality, a sure foundation upon which other things are built. It is not imaginary, but a solid certainty of that for which we hope.

Faith is also "the evidence of things not seen." Evidence implies a thought in belief that is cross-examined and questioned. Faith, then, has proven itself in unquestionable examination.

But what about the unseen? Is it not the power of God working in all events to reveal himself to us? Is it not the revelation of an ultimate and dependable Father who steps in when the going is rough and heavy?

It is this faith that unleashes power for this day.

OSCAR F. REED
Escondido, Calif.
Teacher, Minister

59

This is why I tell you; do not be worried about the food and drink you need in order to stay alive, or about clothes for your body. After all, isn't life worth more than food? And isn't the body worth more than clothes?

(MATT. 6:25, TEV)

Glad It Was Yesterday

Yesterday was "one of those days." From today's perspective, I'm glad it was yesterday.

Since we plan to move, we have our house for sale. The real estate broker called at 8:30 that someone wanted to see the house at 11 A.M. Everybody in the house became unnerved, including myself.

In the rush I forgot to shave. My coffee at breakfast was too hot and spilled over the table. At lunch with a friend I asked for Tabasco sauce. The waitress brought me a large bottle three-fourths full because she "could not find a small one." I, not knowing that it was broken at the base, put it on the table. Half of the contents spilled all over. I noticed it when I felt it on my jacket and trousers. In the evening I locked myself out of my car going to a place of business. Under a heavy rain returning home, I was within a hair of having a terrible accident. I was so glad when upon retiring, I repeated like a baby, "Now I lay me down to sleep," etc.

Small things? Yes. It could happen to anybody? Sure. But why to me when I deserved better? Maybe I was worrying too much. They say, "Worry is the interest we pay on a loan that might never be made."

In retrospect, I have promised not to let small things bother me. Does not God have "the whole world in His hands"?

H. T. REZA
Kansas City
Pastor, Educator, Missions Coordinator, Author

Now give me this hill country that the Lord promised me that day. You yourself heard then that the Anakites were there and their cities were large and fortified, but, the Lord helping me, I will drive them out just as he said.

(JOSH. 14:12)

Caleb's Retirement Attitude

Caleb was 85 years young. He could have been a bitter, sour old man, resentful toward man and God. He could have dwelt on "what might have been" 45 years earlier at Kadesh-barnea. Lesser souls might have washed their hands of this new kingdom project, saying, "I've done my part." Instead, Caleb chose to claim God's unchanging promises.

Through 45 wilderness years Caleb had maintained his faith, vision, and physical conditioning. He now applied for his toughest assignment, believing that, "the Lord helping me," he could overcome every enemy and obstacle.

Caleb well knew that the giant "sons of Anak" (Num. 13:33) still headquartered in Hebron. He knew that this walled city had been bypassed during Joshua's recent Canaan conquests.

Caleb's request was granted. He fought and won his battle. Hebron became his retirement home. His children followed his example by claiming their own promised portions. Providentially, Hebron was later chosen as Israel's most famous "city of refuge."

"Lord, give us a double portion of Caleb's spirit as we challenge our personal giants and walled cities."

GEORGE RICE
Lenexa, Kans.
Minister, NPH Representative

It is a good thing to give thanks unto the Lord,
and to sing praises unto thy name, O most High:
to shew forth thy lovingkindness in the morning,
and thy faithfulness every night.

(PS. 92:1-2)

A Right Perspective

I like to begin every day quoting this psalm to myself—even before I get out of bed. One of the signs of old age is that everything hurts and what doesn't hurt doesn't work. Getting out of bed in retirement years is a good reminder that we aren't getting any younger day by day.

We are so influenced by our feelings that it is easy to fall into the trap of complaining rather than thanking and praising. Evidently the Psalmist had experienced enough ups and downs in life that he had learned the value of giving thanks and praise every day.

Someone taught me years ago that we can complain about a bottle of milk being half empty, or we can rejoice that it is still half full. The circumstance is the same, but we determine whether it will be bad or good. God has given us the ability to make this decision.

If we thank God and rejoice every morning, we will be aware of His faithfulness every night. It's God's Word. It works!

KENNETH S. RICE
Naples, Fla.
Minister

Giving thanks always for all things unto God and the Father
in the name of our Lord Jesus Christ.

(EPH. 5:20)

In All Things

The story is told of a man who lost his leg in an accident. He was taken to the hospital, where a team of doctors performed the necessary surgery to save his life. After the man regained consciousness, the surgeon said to him, "It is very unfortunate that this should have happened to you."

The man responded, "Oh, it might have been worse. I am so thankful it was the leg with rheumatism."

Day by day we experience God's mercies in the midst of the known and the unknown. Let us give thanks—

—not for the pain but for His presence
   —not for sadness but for His solace
      —not for privation but for His provision

Let's look for Him in all things. One word dominated Paul's prayer: *thanks* for what we have in Christ.

"Father, I am thankful."

GILBERT A. RUSHFORD
San Bernardino, Calif.
Pastor

Jesus said, "Let the little children come to me, and do not hinder them, for the kingdom of heaven belongs to such as these." When he had placed his hands on them, he went on from there.

(MATT. 19:14-15, NIV)

The Past Lessons

A senior adult devotional, and he writes about children!

Dr. H. Orton Wiley, college president and Nazarene theologian, used to say, "How can you know how far you've come if you don't remember where you've been?"

Remember when Jesus came into your life? I was nine years of age. Mrs. Jarrette Aycock was holding children's meetings during camp meeting in Nampa, Idaho. Clearly saved at the altar, I could hardly put my feet down walking outside the tent afterward.

But in my teens I fell away. In my senior year of high school, February 16, 1936, at Pasadena College chapel, I was blessedly reclaimed. Three years later, March 9, 1939, the Lord said to me, "Are you really willing to do My will?" Oh, it was the ministry. I was preparing to be a doctor. At Bresee Church altar, a deep "Yes!" brought assurance and sanctification.

Through 50 years—seven pastorates and four years of retirement—the commitment paid!

Look back today. Remember—but look ahead. "When he had placed his hands on them, he went on from there."

HAROLD M. SANNER
Ontario, Oreg.
Pastor

Buy the truth, and sell it not.
(PROV. 23:23)

A Most Important Purchase

Truth needs no correction. It is always right in the long run; and as Dr. J. B. Chapman used to say, "That's the run we are on."

Truth is practical. A father found a favorite cherry tree hacked and ruined. He cried sternly to his son, "George, do you know who did this?"

George looked at his father with quivering lips and said, "Father, I can't tell a lie. I did it."

"Alas!" said the father, "my beautiful tree is ruined; but I had rather lose all the trees I own than to have a liar for a son." The boy who feared a lie more than punishment later became the hero of his country, the great Gen. George Washington, and the first president of his beloved homeland, America.

There is also doctrinal truth. We must purchase it with our heart, soul, and mind. Some like to say that it doesn't matter what you believe just as long as you are sincere about it. Christ said, "I am the way, the truth, and the life" (John 14:6). We must purchase Christ, the Prince of Truth. The truth must be purchased and never sold! If we do sell it, we lose our greatest bargain.

LINDON L. SCALES
Sheffield, Ala.
Minister

I beseech you therefore, brethren, by the mercies of God, that ye present your bodies a living sacrifice, holy, acceptable unto God, which is your reasonable service. And be not conformed to this world: but be ye transformed by the renewing of your mind, that ye may prove what is that good, and acceptable, and perfect, will of God.

(ROM. 12:1-2)

Badges of Devotions

Thomas Kenworthy, "confessed Quaker and recusant," a character in James A. Michener's *Chesapeake,** had been repeatedly flogged by the sheriffs of colonial Massachusetts for his religious nonconformity. When on trial again, with his exposed "back a network of small scars," the presiding judge asked: "Are you aware, Thomas Kenworthy, how your back looks?" The prisoner replied: "I feel it each night before I go to sleep. It is a badge of my devotion to God."

This humble member of the Society of Friends was not a religious exhibitionist. External badges of devotion to God, such as his, are not necessarily objects of our spiritual quest. Most frequently, this badge is likely to be unheralded acts of compassionate caring in the name of our blessed Lord. It may take the form of the spirit of encouragement given to some struggling, discouraged disciple. Or it could be a prayer partner relationship of intercessory prayer for urgent human needs. This kind of religious exercise never calls attention to personal saintliness.

Joyful corporate worship, reinforced by moral and spiritual consistency in the home, community, church, and on the job, never goes unnoticed by our Heavenly Father, which makes earthly accolades pale into insignificance.

*(New York: Fawcett Crest, 1978).

J. RAY SHADOWENS
Spring, Tex.
Minister

For he shall give his angels charge over thee,
to keep thee in all thy ways.
(PS. 91:11)

Angels

Angels, guard me when I'm weary; give me strength for
the road ahead.

Go before me, mark the journey; I can follow if I am led.

Divert me from hidden dangers, provide a shelter in the
storm;

Bind my wounds when sharp swords bleed me, defend
me when temptations swarm.

There are many yawning chasms; escort me, leave me not
alone.

Swing the lantern at the detours, walk with me through
the great unknown.

Feed me, angels, when I'm hungry; nourish every part,
feed the whole.

The flesh is so satiated that I need manna for my soul.

Bring me purple grapes from Eshcol, and pour out honey
from the Rock;

Make me like those early Christians who first stood up at
Antioch

And testified of renewal, freedom from the mundane and
smug.

Give me meat I've never tasted, water from wells I've
never dug.

C. HASTINGS SMITH
Bethany, Okla.
Evangelist

The kingdom of heaven is like treasure hidden in a field.
When a man found it, he hid it again, and then in his joy
went and sold all he had and bought that field.

(MATT. 13:44, NIV)

Hidden Treasure

Those of us who in our youth heard the gospel of Christ, followed instructions, and sold all our worldly treasure and ambition in order to follow Christ, know the truth of this parable. The kingdom of heaven is full of hidden treasure! Now in the later years of our lives we are sustained continually by the spiritual dividends paid for this great investment.

Satan tried to tell us we would lose all. We have found instead that our lives have been saved for time and eternity. Daily we experience the joy of sins forgiven. Our souls have rest while serving Christ and the church. What "the Lord, the righteous Judge," has laid up for us will be glorious (2 Tim. 4:8, NIV).

While the devil has no happy old men or women, those who serve Christ and His Church down to old age find daily happiness. Also, we have found, "The path of the righteous is like the first gleam of dawn, shining ever brighter till the full light of day" (Prov. 4:18, NIV).

PAUL M. SODOWSKY
Oklahoma City
Minister

*Yet I am not ashamed, because I know whom I have believed,
and am convinced that he is able to guard what I have
entrusted to him for that day.*

(2 TIM. 1:12, NIV)

"Know-So" Faith

Nazarenes used to talk about "know-so" salvation. Knowing one was saved was very important. Knowing Christ was also important to Paul.

A beautiful illustration of this comes from Swaziland. A preacher's old father was visited one day by his preacher son, who decided to test his father's faith and commitment to the Lord. "Father," he said, "what would you do if the Nazarene missionaries came one day and told you they had been teaching nothing but lies all these years?"

After deep thought, his father said, "Son, if that ever happens, I will know one thing—I will know that all the Nazarene missionaries are backslidden. God has been too real and has done too much for me to doubt Him now. Even if the missionaries who brought me the message were to tell me it isn't true, it would not shake me. Don't worry, Son, I am going to stay true."

That is "know-so"! Stay true he did and today he is with his Lord.

D. HERMAN SPENCER
Lakewood, Colo.
Missionary

That was the true Light, which lighteth every man
that cometh into the world.

(JOHN 1:9)

Just in Case

On Christmas Eve, 1944, our overseas orders were miraculously delayed. Therefore, I received a three-day pass to go home for Christmas. As trains and buses were overloaded, I had to hitchhike. We got lost in a fierce snowstorm and ended up in Kingman, Kans., west of Wichita, my hometown.

At 2 A.M. I got a ride in a poultry truck that would only go 30 m.p.h. With turkey feathers flying and snow swirling around us, what did I care? I was going home for Christmas.

At 4 A.M. I stepped out in heavy snow five blocks from home. Every house was bathed in darkness. Just as I turned the corner, I saw one Christmas light, and it was in our front window.

What a surprised family and happy homecoming! After all the hugs and greetings I asked my dad, "Why did you have that one little Christmas light burning in the window?" His answer stirred me then and thrills me still: "Just in case one of our three soldier boys might come home for Christmas . . . Just in case!"

Almost 2,000 years ago God put a light in heaven's window . . . "Just in case."

SAM STEARMAN
Bethany, Okla.
Pastor, Founder of NIROGA

Jesus said unto him, Thou shalt love the Lord thy God with all thy heart, and with all thy soul, and with all thy mind.

(MATT. 22:37)

More than Molecules

Man is made of DNA (deoxyribonucleic acid). Our very lives are locked in the nuclei of a hundred trillion cells. The secrets of life lie inside each cell in chemical molecules of strands of DNA.

Basically DNA is similar in animals and plants. In man a great difference exists. "God said, Let us make man in our image" (Gen. 1:26). DNA is present plus the soul. Christ has infused us with spiritual life that is just as real as natural life. Man can carry within his body the literal presence of Deity. Just as the human code is present in each body cell in DNA, God permeates the living soul with His presence.

This brings a sobering responsibility. "What? know ye not that your body is the temple of the Holy Ghost which is in you, which ye have of God, and ye are not your own? For ye are bought with a price" (1 Cor. 6:19-20). Therefore love God with all your heart and mind plus your soul. A Christian is triune, made up of body, mind, and everlasting spirit. It's wonderful to know that we were made in the image of God.

DWIGHT J. STRICKLER
Bourbonnais, Ill.
Professor of Biological Science

For the which cause I also suffer these things: nevertheless I am not ashamed: for I know whom I have believed, and am persuaded that he is able to keep that which I have committed unto him against that day.

(2 TIM. 1:12)

Uncertainties

Fear and bitterness are the twin perils of old age. No one had more reason to be afraid or to be bitter than the apostle Paul as he wrote these words from a prison in Rome. He knew he would soon be violently killed at Nero's hands. And in his hour of deepest need he had been deserted by his friends (see 4:10-16).

But Paul was neither fearful nor bitter. Why? Because the closest and mightiest friend was still right there with him—Jesus. He had already, long before, committed to Jesus his sins, his fears, his perplexities, his disappointments, and all the cruel things others had done to him. Therefore none of those things bothered him now. He was free and at peace. Let us know Jesus—really *know* Him—closely and intimately. Then we will not be shaken or frightened even by the uncertainties of old age.

RICHARD S. TAYLOR
Portland, Oreg.
Minister, Teacher

For as the lightning cometh out of the east, and shineth even unto the west; so shall also the coming of the Son of man be.
(MATT. 24:27)

Peace in the Storm

During my early childhood, late one June afternoon, a great summer thunderstorm swept over us. The family gathered inside until the wind, the lightning, and the thunder abated.

As soon as it was over, the father, mother, and children gathered on the long front porch to enjoy the beautiful evening. Not a leaf was stirring. The sparrows began to chirp. The birds, as well as the chickens, moved about across the yard seeking bugs, insects, and worms. No one spoke a word, and a sense of great calmness and peace settled on my boyish mind.

Just then, there came a flash of lightning. It made me uneasy. Father looked at me and said, "Have no fear —the lightning is from the east. When the lightning is from the east, the storm has passed over." Later in life I read Matt. 24:27 and remembered that when Jesus comes, the storm is over. When the storm passes over and Jesus comes, there will be peace, serenity, and perfect joy.

C. R. THRASHER
Nashville
Minister

And the prayer of faith shall save the sick, and the Lord shall raise him up; and if he have committed sins, they shall be forgiven him. Confess your faults one to another, and pray one for another, that ye may be healed. The effectual fervent prayer of a righteous man availeth much.
(JAMES 5:15-16)

Healing Faith

A bivocational pastor in Kentucky visited his physician after nursing what he thought was bronchitis for some time. A careful analysis of his blood test resulted in a diagnosis of acute leukemia. Immediate, heavy doses of chemotherapy threw his body into a total coma for seven weeks.

The district emergency prayer chain was activated. Pastors and laypeople far and wide earnestly pled for his healing. As his district superintendent, I anointed him with oil. His wife and mine joined hands and faith with us as we prayed. The specialist in charge of his case declared, "Let it be known that if this man recovers, it will not be because of anything medical science has done!"

Eighteen months later, in the pink of health, following a complete examination, that same specialist declared, "Reverend, if I hadn't been connected with your case, no one could convince me that you ever suffered from leukemia."

Who touched the throne for him? Who offered the prayer of faith? Who cares! The fact is, *someone did.* And God fulfilled His promise. "The effectual fervent prayer of [the] righteous . . . availeth much." Do you qualify? Then exercise your privilege and trust God to minister to the needs of people.

ALECK G. ULMET
Bella Vista, Ark.
Pastor, District Superintendent, Evangelist

74

He . . . will enlarge the harvest of your [faithfulness].
(2 COR. 9:10, NIV)

Faithfulness Speaks

Years ago I sought a loan from a banker for the building of a new worship complex. After I explained who I was and the need of my church for thousands of dollars, he replied, "So you are a Nazarene." Then he continued, "I used to live in Fairbanks, Alaska. I had a large, beautiful home with a picture window in the front. I watched a group of people building a tar-paper-sided church down on the corner. It was bitter cold, but day after day these dedicated folk worked at their task."

And then he added, "Although I didn't agree with their faith or belief, I did say they surely must love their God; and Reverend, on the strength of the Nazarenes in Fairbanks, Alaska, 25 years ago, I will loan you all the money you need."

Today there are two beautiful churches where hundreds of people come to worship. One in Fairbanks, Alaska, and the other in Phoenix.

Our faithfulness to God today could mean that others in the tomorrows might reap a harvest too.

CRAWFORD VANDERPOOL
Prescott, Ariz.
Minister

75

Teach us to number our days aright,
that we may gain a heart of wisdom.
(PS. 90:12, NIV)

The righteous will flourish . . . They will still bear fruit
in old age, they will stay fresh and green.
(PS. 92:12, 14, NIV)

Drive or Dawdle?

Usually when I tee off in golf, it is my intention to drive that little ball farther than ever before in my whole life. Last week when a screaming slice sent my ball far out into the lake, it occurred to me again that at my age I should ease up a bit and not drive so hard.

Medical advice in the 1950s was "to sprint up to 25 years, trot from 25 to 40, walk from 40 to 60, and after 60 you can dawdle with golf."

The "heart of wisdom" in the game of life, as well as golf, is to play it somewhere between the extremes of "drive" and "dawdle," depending on our age and other factors. The weathering seasons tempt us to dawdle in childish, critical, distrustful behavior. To dawdle with excesses of eating, entertainment, and ease. "There's no fool like an old fool." Paul says, "Teach the older men to be temperate, worthy of respect, self-controlled, and sound in faith, in love and in endurance. Likewise, teach the older women to be reverent in the way they live, . . ." (Titus 2:2-3, NIV).

WILFORD N. VANDERPOOL
Sun Lakes, Ariz.
Minister

Fear thou not; for I am with thee: be not dismayed; for I am thy God: I will strengthen thee; yea, I will help thee; yea, I will uphold thee.

(ISA. 41:10)

I am he that liveth, and was dead; and, behold, I am alive for evermore, Amen; and have the keys of hell and of death.

(REV. 1:18)

Holding Steady

It seems that every morning we face some new tragic headline: natural disaster, man-made tragedies, political upheavals—any of which could affect our lives at any time!

Yet we Christians affirm, "We believe in God the Father Almighty, Maker of heaven and earth." We sing from our hearts, "Faith is the victory / That overcomes the world!" It's a faith that assures us God is in control, that the raging "nations are as a drop in a bucket" to Him (Isa. 40:15, NKJV), and that we are not left without power and direction for our lives.

But this faith doesn't just rise from nowhere. It firmly rests upon what happened at Calvary. God gave His Son to bear our sin and suffering, and to confront all the agents of evil. They did their utmost. They put Him to death on a cross. The verdict was: Crucified, dead, and buried—nothing more final than that. Nevertheless, on the first day of the week He arose, a victor over the dark domain of sin and death. *He lives!* And that faith keeps us steady.

EUGENE R. VERBECK
Colorado Springs
Pastor

I tell you that if two of you on earth agree about anything you ask for, it will be done for you by my Father in heaven. For where two or three come together in my name, there am I with them.

(MATT. 18:19-20, NIV)

Gathered in Jesus' Name

One who was very profane in using the Lord's name was asked: "How much does the devil pay you to swear?" It's true that no name is so abused as the wonderful name of Jesus, yet no name is so precious or powerful.

As we gather in His name, we have the guarantee of His presence. Sometimes we pray for Him to come and meet with us, but that is unnecessary if we gather in His name. In the words of Livingstone: "His word is that of a gentleman." Since we have no credit in the Bank of Heaven, we ask in His name, for He alone is worthy.

I like to think of those early Christians in the catacombs, although it is easy to idealize their situation from our vantage point. I like to think about Paul and Luke and Timothy on those weary roads of Europe and Asia Minor. They were weak and human, but Jesus was with them; and because they went in His name, they were invincible. In His name is all the concentrated power of eternal life.

VERNON L. WILCOX
Nampa, Idaho
Pastor

*The path of the just is as the shining light, that shineth
more and more unto the perfect day.*
(PROV. 4:18)

The Brighter Pathway

In the flood-city of western Pennsylvania, I opened my heart to the Light of the World. And He has guided me on life's journey.

At eight years of age, however, I hadn't yet tested the great promises of God. But Joshua had. And in his farewell message to the leaders of Israel he said, "You know with all your heart and soul that not one of all the good promises the Lord your God gave you has failed" (Josh. 23:14, NIV).

Throughout my pilgrimage and into these retirement years, I, too, have learned that God's promises never fail.

As a lad of eight, my faith had not been tested and tried. Veteran Paul, however, had met life's challenges. In his last testimony he wrote, "I have fought a good fight, I have finished my course, I have kept the faith" (2 Tim. 4:7).

I, too, have kept the faith. The crises and challenges of the passing years have not put out the light. In fact, the pathway grows brighter. And, by God's unfailing grace, I shall see that city where night never comes.

EARL C. WOLF
Hazelwood, Mo.
Pastor, Writer, Editor, Administrator